THE WRITER SYSTEM NOTEBOOK

A Methodical Approach to Outlining Your Novel

ALLAN L MANN

Copyright © 2019 Allan L. Mann

All rights reserved. No part of this book may be reproduced, or stored in a retrieval system, or transmitted in any form or by any means, electronic, mechanical, photocopying, recording, or otherwise, without express written permission of the author, except for the use of brief quotations in a book review.

First edition November 2019

Author photograph by Allan L Mann

Library of Congress Control Number: 2019910275

ISBN 978-1-7329227-4-7

Published by: Noir Café Press, LLC

www.NoirCafePress.com

"The first draft is just you telling yourself the story."

Terry Pratchett

"The process of doing your second draft is a process of making it look like you knew what you were doing all along."

Neil Gaiman

Index

Project Details	1
Publishing Targets	3
The WRITER System	7

Using the WRITER System

Part 1 — Outlining	11
Part 2 — Working Plot Thread	15
Part 3 — The 4-Act Structure	17

Part I
Outlining

World	22
Rival	30
Idol	36
Twists	42
End	48
Resolve	54
Synopsis and Questions	61
Synopsis #1	62
Questions from Synopsis #1	63
Synopsis #2	64
Questions from Synopsis #2	66
Synopsis #3	68
Questions from Synopsis #3	72
Synopsis #4	76
Questions from Synopsis #4	82
Synopsis #5	88

Part II
Working Plot Thread

Main Plot Arc	98
Subplots	104

Character Arcs	108

Part III
The 4-Act Structure

Act 1 - Preparation	114
Act 2 - Reaction	120
Act 3 - Proaction	126
Act 4 - Conclusion	132

Sketches

People

Protagonist:	142
Antagonist:	144
Sidekick:	146
Character:	148
Character:	150
Character:	152
Character:	154
Character:	156

Places

Location:	160
Location:	162
Location:	164
Location:	166
Location:	168
Location:	170
Location:	172
Location:	174
Research Notes	176
Freestyle	196
Resources	236
About the Author	239

Project Details

Title:

Subtitle:

Author:

Publication Date:

Publishing Targets
3 TIMELINES TO PUBLISH YOUR BOOK

Outline

1 Year — 3 weeks:
6 Months — 10 days:
100 Days — 3 days:

Rough First Draft

1 Year — 4 months:
6 Months — 2 months:
100 Days — 1 month:

Final First Draft

1 Year — 1 month:
6 Months — 2 weeks:
100 Days — 2 days:

Edit One

3 weeks:

Edit Two

3 weeks:

Final Proof

10 days:

Formatting

Professional — 2 weeks:
Self — 3 days:

Advanced Reader Team

2 weeks before Soft Launch:

Soft Launch

Friday before Hard Launch:

Hard Launch

Release on a Monday or Tuesday:

Release Party!

The WRITER System

Thank you for being a writer, an author. The world is made all the more joyful, entertaining, and exciting with your creations in it.

As an author, I love creating, but I also enjoy the creative process — how an author writes. As I wrote my first three stories, I quickly came to understand my working process.

People say there are two types of writers — *pantsers* and *plotters*. That seemed very black and white to me. On the one hand, you have those who sit at the keyboard and write the story as if they're watching a movie play out in their mind's eye. On the other, some authors like to plot out every last move of their characters. And never the twain shall meet. I think the reality for many, however, lies somewhere in between.

And that's where **THE WRITER SYSTEM** began.

WRITER stands for World, Rival, Idol, Twists, End, and Resolve.

Each one of these elements will help you craft the big picture of your next novel. From this basic Outline, you'll create ever-more detailed Synopsis by questioning each point within it. From the final Synopsis, a 4-Act Structure is developed, hitting all of the beat points required of a good story.

Other elements included in this planner are scene and character sketches, plot and character arcs, notes on scene construction, a writing timeline tool (or the dreaded deadline!).

There is *plenty* of space for your notes in each section and several pages at the end of this notebook for your moments of inspiration on the fly.

I hope you enjoy using this tool in your writing, and I'd love to hear if you have any feedback or suggestions on how to make this an even more useful resource.

Allan L Mann
Georgetown, KY, July 2019

Using the WRITER System

The layout that follows is based on what I call the WRITER System. In fact, WRITER is only part of a more comprehensive system for planning and plotting your novel. Please use all or part of the system or adjust it to make it useful in your daily writing regime.

The **WRITER System** consists of 3 main parts:

1. Outlining.
2. Working Plot Thread.
3. 4-Act Structure.

Each section builds your plot outline to the point you can begin writing the first draft of your story.

Part 1 – Outlining

Starting out, you most likely have a general idea of the story you want to tell – the very rough beginning, middle and end. Step 1, Outlining, allows you to capture the basic information of your story. It begins with the W.R.I.T.E.R. System and moves into crafting the basic premise of the story.

The W.R.I.T.E.R. System

World. Describe, in broad strokes, where your story takes place. If writing fiction, this can be made easier by "writing what you know" and basing the story in a location you're familiar with. If you're creating a world for something like a science fiction story, start again with what you know - what other books/movies come to mind when you think of your world, then develop it from there. Don't be afraid to create imaginary locations based on real life. For example, in the real world there may just be a field in this particular location, but for the purposes of your story you need a factory there. Go for it!

Rival. Your villain or antagonist - the Bad Guy. With

whom (or what) is your protagonist going to be battling? It's good to figure out who the bad guy is going to be. A strong antagonist is key to a good story. If that antagonist is a person, then make them believable. Craft them in such a way that you can sympathise on some level with them or their goals.

Idol. Your hero or protagonist - the Good Guy. What does he/she have to lose? What are the internal and external conflicts?

Twists. The 3 Game-changers that move the story on in each act, plus the ultimate Act 4 twist in the tail.

End. What is the end game? The Idol and Rival meet.

Resolve. Have you answered all of the questions posed in the story? If not, can the reader expect an answer (in a follow-up story)? What are the holes in the story? Fix them!

Now you have the basic ideas listed, move on to creating the Premise.

Premise

The Premise is split into 2 sections – the **Synopsis** and **Questions** – which circle back on each other as you build in more details.

Synopsis & Questions

Start short - very short - then expand. Before you go through this exercise, you already have a bigger picture - a more complete story arc - in mind. However, start small and expand. What is the absolute shortest way to describe the story? Start by trying to write the hook for your book listing on Amazon. As an example, we'll use the details from my novel, TOOLS OF THE TRADE.

Synopsis #1:

A clothing company loses their head of R&D - tied to the cliffs below the high tide line. The investigation uncovers a web of lies and cover-ups.

Now, go to the Questions page and ask as many questions posed by Synopsis #1:

What clothing company?

Ogilvy Outerwear.

Where is the company located?

Arbroath.

What do they make?

Primarily outdoor activity clothing, but also foul weather jackets for Police Scotland.

Who dies?

Bobby Want, Director of R&D.

What lies and cover-ups?

Owners and employees of the company keep back details from the investigators.

Who are the main characters at Ogilvy?

Ogilvy, MD

Daughter, receptionist.

Brother-in-law, executive.

Who is investigating?

Tom Guthrie.

Does this cause conflict with the local police station?

Yes. Former CID partner runs Arbroath.

Who is this?

Inspector Ian Buchanan.

Who else is on the team?

Alisdair McEwan - young PC. Etc., etc.

Take all of these answers and use them to create Synopsis #2.

Synopsis #2:

The head of R&D for Ogilvy Outerwear, Bobby Gant, is found tied to the cliffs below the high tide line in Arbroath. Tom Guthrie, a retired detective sergeant, is called in by a resource-strapped Police Scotland to help lead investigation, much to the annoyance of his former CID partner, now boss of the local station, Ian Buchanan. Guthrie is tasked with solving the murder, as well as looking after a young, over-enthusiastic PC assigned to the inquiry. They quickly realize that the owners of the clothing company are holding back details from them.

Repeat the exercise:

Did the killers want him to be found? Why?

How did Guthrie retire?

Why is Police Scotland asking a retired officer to come back on a murder case?

Why are they resource-strapped?

What's the history between Guthrie and Buchanan? Why would Buchanan be annoyed? What's PC McEwan's personality?

What details are being held back?

Write Synopsis #3: Synopsis #3: ???? Questions.

Synopsis #4: ???? Questions.

Synopsis #5: ????

Once you hit at least Synopsis #5, you're ready to move onto the next part of the **WRITER** System.

Part 2 – Working Plot Thread

Plot Arc

Using the last Synopsis you created, outline your plot. Break down the synopsis into the 4 Acts of the story — Preparation, Ruction, Proaction, Conclusion. You'll use these as the starting point for the 4-Act Structure section later on.

From our Synopsis:

[PREPARATION: The head of R&D for Ogilvy Outerwear, Bobby Gant, is found tied to the cliffs below the high tide line in Arbroath.]

[REACTION: Tom Guthrie, a retired detective sergeant, is called in by a resource-strapped Police Scotland to help lead investigation, much to the annoyance of his former CID partner, now boss of the local station, Ian Buchanan. Guthrie is tasked with solving the murder, as well as looking after a young, over-enthusiastic PC Alisdair McEwan, assigned to the inquiry. They quickly realize that the owners of the clothing company are holding back details from them. In the meantime a fire at a warehouse kills a homeless man. This is added to Guthrie's plate.]

[PROACTION: Guthrie decides to pressure Ogilvy and take

charge of matters in his own way. He pressures Ogilvy for answers. The warehouse fire is tied up quickly and things seem to be going well when Alisdair goes missing.]

[CONCLUSION: Everything comes to a head on a rain-soaked evening at the harbor, when Guthrie must rescue Alisdair and the real murderer.]

Bookmark this section – we'll be coming back to it soon. But first, let's briefly talk about the people in our story.

Character Arcs

This section is for you to take on-going notes about each of your characters. As with the story itself, each character's journey must have a beginning, middle and end. Your central characters must change as your novel progresses. As you work through telling your story, keep adding notes about each character. This is a handy place to catalogue all the details related to them.

Part 3 — The 4-Act Structure

This is where we begin to structure the story — logically laying out the 4 Acts.

Act 1 - Preparation - 20% (of total word count)

Plot Point 1 — Inciting Incident

Game-changer 1 — Plot Point 2 — Lock-in

First Transition

Act 2 - Reaction - 25%

Game-changer 2 — Plot Point 3 — First Culmination

Second Transition

Act 3 - Proaction - 25%

Game-changer 3 – Plot Point 4 – Main Culmination

Third Transition

Act 4 - Conclusion - 30%

Climax – Plot Point 5

Pay-off 1

Twist – Plot Point 6

Rush

Pay-off 2

I've listed each beat of the story "graphically" as the story builds, your Idol has some initial wins, the Rival gets the upper hand, then builds again towards the Climax and Twist, before settling back down at the End and you Resolve the plot.

Rewind to Step 2 and the Plot Arc. Take each of the colour-coded sections in the Synopsis and break those down further, matching each beat point with the appropriate beat point within the 4 Act Structure. Make sure you have something for each beat of the story (12 in all).

By the way, the percentages indicate, roughly, how much of the story should be contained in each Act. Purely a suggestion!

What's next? Well, we write!

Everything you've done so far is designed to make the task of writing your story easier. If the story is the cake, then the WRITER System is the gathering of the ingredients, the recipe to make sure you're not forgetting the flour or the butter. Use it now to help guide you through your story.

Just as we began with a 2-sentence Synopsis, and then expanded it through several rewrites, take each beat within the 4-Act Structure and begin writing the first draft. Because you have all of these plot points lined up, the writing should be easier – you know where you're going. Having said this, don't feel as though you have to stick to your notes so rigidly you can't be creative. If your Idol wants to turn left instead of right, that's exactly what he/she needs to do.

Enjoy the ride!

PART I

Outlining

World
WHERE DOES YOUR STORY TAKE PLACE?

World

World

World

World

Rival

YOUR VILLAIN OR ANTAGONIST - THE BAD GUY.

Rival

Rival

Rival

Idol

YOUR HERO OR PROTAGONIST – THE GOOD GUY.

Idol

Idol

Idol

Twists

THE 3 GAME-CHANGERS THAT MOVE THE STORY ON IN EACH ACT, PLUS THE ULTIMATE ACT 4 TWIST IN THE TAIL.

Twists

Twists

Twists

End

WHAT IS THE END GAME? THE IDOL AND RIVAL MEET.

End

End

End

Resolve

HAVE YOU ANSWERED ALL OF THE QUESTIONS POSED IN THE STORY?

Resolve

Resolve

Resolve

Synopsis and Questions

Synopsis #1

THE ONE- OR TWO-SENTENCE MINI SYNOPSIS.

Questions from Synopsis #1

ALL THE QUESTIONS RAISED BY SYNOPSIS #1, AND THE ANSWERS.

Synopsis #2

WRITE A NEW SYNOPSIS, INCLUDING THE DETAIL PROVIDED BY THE Q&A FROM THE PREVIOUS STEP.

Synopsis #2

Questions from Synopsis #2

ALL THE QUESTIONS RAISED BY SYNOPSIS #2, AND THE ANSWERS.

Questions from Synopsis #2

Synopsis #3

WRITE A NEW SYNOPSIS, INCLUDING THE DETAIL PROVIDED BY THE Q&A FROM THE PREVIOUS STEP.

Synopsis #3

Synopsis #3

Questions from Synopsis #3

ALL THE QUESTIONS RAISED BY SYNOPSIS #3, AND THE ANSWERS.

Questions from Synopsis #3

Questions from Synopsis #3

Synopsis #4

WRITE A NEW SYNOPSIS, INCLUDING THE DETAIL PROVIDED BY THE Q&A FROM THE PREVIOUS STEP.

Synopsis #4

Synopsis #4

Synopsis #4

Questions from Synopsis #4

ALL THE QUESTIONS RAISED BY SYNOPSIS #4, AND THE ANSWERS.

Questions from Synopsis #4

Questions from Synopsis #4

Questions from Synopsis #4

Synopsis #5

WRITE YOUR FINAL SYNOPSIS, INCLUDING THE DETAIL PROVIDED BY THE Q&A FROM THE PREVIOUS STEP.

Synopsis #5

Synopsis #5

Synopsis #5

Synopsis #5

PART II

Working Plot Thread

Main Plot Arc

Main Plot Arc

Main Plot Arc

Main Plot Arc

Subplots

Subplots

Subplots

Character Arcs

Character Arcs

Character Arcs

PART III

The 4-Act Structure

Act 1 - Preparation
20%

Plot Point 1 – Inciting Incident

    Game-changer 1 – Plot Point 2 – Lock-in

            First Transition

Act 1

Act 1

Act 1

Act 2 - Reaction

25%

Game-changer 2 – Plot Point 3 – First Culmination

Second Transition

Act 2

Act 2

Act 2

Act 3 - Proaction

25%

Game-changer 3 – Plot Point 4 – Main Culmination

Third Transition

Act 3

Act 3

Act 3

Act 4 - Conclusion
30%

Climax – Plot Point 5

        Pay-off 1

                Twist – Plot Point 6

                    Rush

        Pay-off 2

Act 4

Act 4

Act 4

Sketches

IN THIS SECTION YOU'LL FIND SOME TEMPLATES FOR OUTLINING THE CHARACTERS AND IMPORTANT LOCATIONS IN YOUR STORY.

People

Protagonist:

ROLE IN STORY:

Physical Description/Mannerisms:

Personality:

Background:

Conflicts:

Notes:

Protagonist

_____

Antagonist:
_____

ROLE IN STORY:

Physical Description/Mannerisms:

Personality:

Background:

Conflicts:

Notes:

Antagonist

_____

Sidekick: _____
_____

ROLE IN STORY:

Physical Description/Mannerisms:

Personality:

Background:

Conflicts:

Notes:

Sidekick

Character:

ROLE IN STORY:

Physical Description/Mannerisms:

Personality:

Background:

Conflicts:

Notes:

Character

Character:

ROLE IN STORY:

Physical Description/Mannerisms:

Personality:

Background:

Conflicts:

Notes:

Character

Character:

ROLE IN STORY:

Physical Description/Mannerisms:

Personality:

Background:

Conflicts:

Notes:

Character

_____

Character:
_____

ROLE IN STORY:

Physical Description/Mannerisms:

Personality:

Background:

Conflicts:

Notes:

Character

Character: _____

ROLE IN STORY:

Physical Description/Mannerisms:

Personality:

Background:

Conflicts:

Notes:

Character

Places

Location:

ROLE IN STORY:

Related Characters:

Season:

Unique Features:

Description:

Notes:

Location

_____

Location:
_____

ROLE IN STORY:

Related Characters:

Season:

Unique Features:

Description:

Notes:

Location

Location:

ROLE IN STORY:

Related Characters:

Season:

Unique Features:

Description:

Notes:

Location

_____

Location:
_____

ROLE IN STORY:

Related Characters:

Season:

Unique Features:

Description:

Notes:

Location

Location:

ROLE IN STORY:

Related Characters:

Season:

Unique Features:

Description:

Notes:

Location

_____

Location:
_____

ROLE IN STORY:

Related Characters:

Season:

Unique Features:

Description:

Notes:

Location

_____

Location:
_____

ROLE IN STORY:

Related Characters:

Season:

Unique Features:

Description:

Notes:

Location

Location:
_____

ROLE IN STORY:

Related Characters:

Season:

Unique Features:

Description:

Notes:

Location

Research Notes

Research Notes

Research Notes

Research Notes

Research Notes

Research Notes

Research Notes

Research Notes

Research Notes

Research Notes

Research Notes

Freestyle

POSSIBILITY PAGES TO CAPTURE YOUR INSPIRATION!

Freestyle

Freestyle

Freestyle

Freestyle

Freestyle

Freestyle

Freestyle

Freestyle

Freestyle

Freestyle

Freestyle

Freestyle

Freestyle

Freestyle

Freestyle

Freestyle

Freestyle

Freestyle

Freestyle

Freestyle

Resources

HERE ARE SOME WONDERFUL RESOURCES FOR INDEPENDENT AUTHORS. I'VE USED THEM ALL.

Publishing

- www.booklinker.net - "Free global/universal short-links for your Amazon content."
www.bitly.com - "URL shortener. Custom branded URLs."
- www.bookfunnel.com - Easy eBook delivery.
- www.draft2digital.com - Platform to easily publish eBooks on various outlets.
www.kdp.amazon.com - "Self-publish eBooks and paperbacks on Amazon for free."
www.mailchimp.com - "Marketing automation platform."

Publishing Advice

- www.thecreativepenn.com - "Resources to help you write, publish and market your book, as well as

- make a living with your writing."
- www.kobowritinglife.com - "A blog about writing and self-publishing." www.reedsy.com - "Find the perfect editor, designer or marketer." www.selfpublishingformula.com - "Make a living with your writing." www.chrisfoxwrites.com – Lots of videos and information (including Scrivener). www.honoreecorder.com – "Stategic book coach."

Other

- www.dropbox.com - "Modern workspace designed to reduce busywork." www.evernote.com - "Organize your notes with Evernote."
- www.literatureandlatte.com - "Tools that embrace the creativity of all kind of composition." www.simplenote.com - "The simplest way to keep notes."
- www.wordpress.com - "Create a free website or blog."

About the Author

Allan grew up on the East coast of Scotland, and has been a professional pilot his entire career. He thought writing books would be much simpler. He was wrong.

His first novel, TOOLS OF THE TRADE, was published as an ebook in 2016, then paperback in 2019.

Allan lives in Georgetown, Kentucky. He and his wife, Christy, have three daughters, Katie, Emily, and Maureen.

www.ingramcontent.com/pod-product-compliance
Lightning Source LLC
Chambersburg PA
CBHW020251030426
42336CB00010B/710